With Th...

Making Gourd Bowls

Sammie Crawford
The Fairy Gourdmother®

4880 Lower Valley Road • Atglen, PA • 19310

Other Schiffer Books by the Author:
Creating Gourd Birds with The Fairy Gourdmother®
978-0-7643-3735-2, $24.99

Building Gourd Birdhouses with The Fairy Gourdmother®
978-0-7643-3736-9, $24.99

Gourd Fun for Everyone
978-0-7643-3124-4, $22.99

Holiday Fun: Painting Christmas Gourds
978-0-7643-3279-1, $14.99

Designed by RoS
Type set in MetaCondBold/Arrus BT
ISBN: 978-0-7643-3980-6

Printed in China

PUBLISHING

Schiffer Books are available at special discounts for bulk purchases for sales promotions or premiums. Special editions, including personalized covers, corporate imprints, and excerpts can be created in large quantities forw special needs. For more information contact the publisher:

Published by Schiffer Publishing Ltd.
4880 Lower Valley Road
Atglen, PA 19310

Phone: (610) 593-1777; Fax: (610) 593-2002
E-mail: Info@schifferbooks.com

For the largest selection of fine reference books on this and related subjects, please visit our web site at:
www.schifferbooks.com

We are always looking for people to write books on new and related subjects. If you have an idea for a book, please contact us at
proposals@schifferbooks.com

This book may be purchased from the publisher.
Include $5.00 for shipping.
Please try your bookstore first.

You may write for a free catalog.

In Europe, Schiffer books are distributed by
Bushwood Books
6 Marksbury Ave.
Kew Gardens
Surrey TW9 4JF England

Phone: 44 (0) 20 8392 8585; Fax: 44 (0) 20 8392 9876
E-mail: info@bushwoodbooks.co.uk
Website: **www.bushwoodbooks.co.uk**

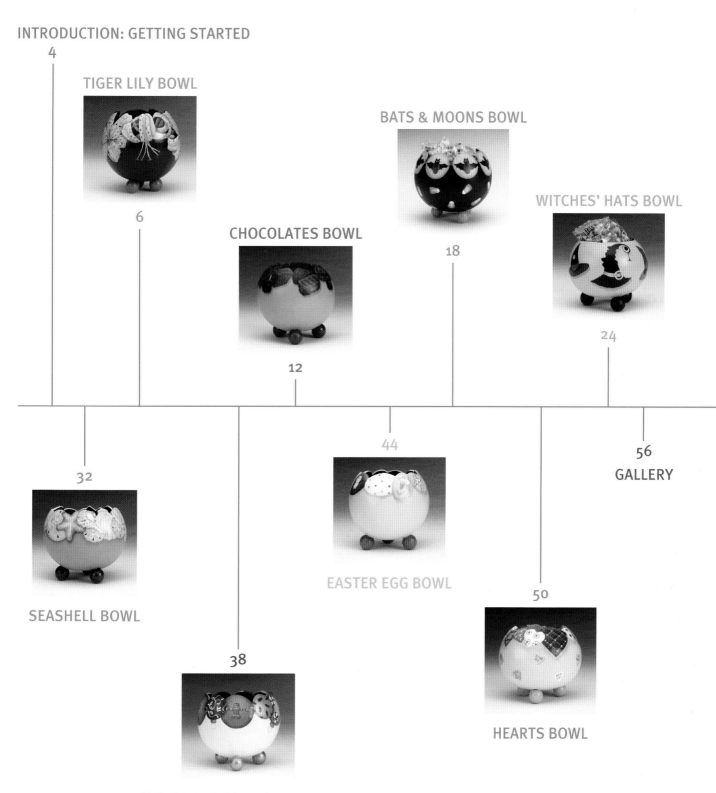

Getting Started

Every gourd is different and because they're different, each pattern in this book will require some sort of adjustment whether it's enlarging or reducing to fit your particular gourd. The best way to apply a flat pattern to a round surface is to cut the pattern tracing into pieces, applying the individual features where needed.

Gourds are almost all water when green. To dry out to the stage where we can use them, all that water has to evaporate through the skin. In the process, they turn black and moldy. This is when first-time growers throw them away, thinking that they are ruined when actually it's just a necessary step in the process.

When they are light and the seeds rattle (usually), it's time to clean all that mold off. Soak them in the sink in a little water and bleach for a few minutes to soften the skin. They float like corks so turn them occasionally to get them wet all over. Use a plastic scrubber; most of the skin will come right off. Remove any stubborn spots with a dull paring knife. Get the gourd completely clean because anything left can flake off later and take all your hard work and paint with it. Once clean and dry, you're ready to paint.

Your "usual painting supplies" should include tracing paper, transfer paper in black and white, palette paper, a divided water tub or two water containers, Q-tips®, good grade paper towels, stylus, palette knife, short flexible ruler, kneaded eraser, sponge, pencils, charcoal, and chalk pencils. Now, you only have to add the brushes and paints you will need and you're ready to go.

MAKING THE BOWLS

All bowls begin the same. Follow these simple steps to getting them level. You must put the feet on **FIRST** or you will probably never get the top level.

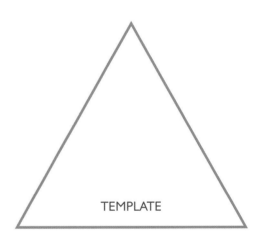

TEMPLATE

1. Use the template pattern to mark the three places to drill.

2. Use the recommended size drill bit to make the three holes. Glue the dowels into the balls and fit them into the holes. If the dowels stick too far into the bowl, shorten them until they're even with the inside surface and then glue them in place.

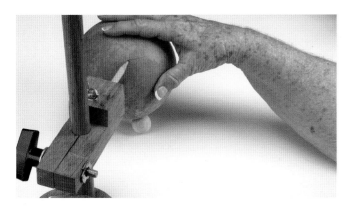

3. Using the level marker, scribe a line around the top of the gourd where you want the opening and then cut the top off.

4. Clean the gourd out real good and make the inside smooth for painting later.

5. Fit the pattern to the rim and trace around it.

6. Use the craft saw to cut away the excess gourd around the top. Now you're ready to paint.

Tiger Lily Bowl

PALETTE

Delta Ceramcoat
- Black
- White
- Calypso Orange
- Poppy Orange
- Georgia Clay
- Butter Cream
- Spice Brown
- Spice Tan
- Light Foliage
- Medium Foliage
- Dark Foliage
- Red Iron Oxide

BRUSHES

Loew-Cornell
- Series 7300 #12 flat shader
- Series 7350 10/0 liner
- Series 7500 #4 filbert
- Series 7550 1" wash brush

SUPPLIES

- Cannonball gourd, 6-8" diameter
- 3 small round wooden knobs
- 3/16" dowel
- 3/16" drill and drill bit
- Craft saw
- Leveling tool
- Wood glue
- Gloss spray varnish

TIGER LILY BOWL

TIGER LILY BOWL PATTERN

ASSEMBLING THE BOWL PAINTING THE BOWL

Follow the initial instructions as described in the Introduction "Making the Bowls." After applying the pattern, if you have space left, you can use some of the lilies more than once. Flip the pattern over to give them a different look if you like. Fill in around the rim with leaves anywhere you may have a gap larger than you like. If pressed for room, let the lilies overlap a little. Cut around the tops of the flowers.

1. Use the wash brush to basecoat the background and inside with Black. Undercoat the flowers with White and base the leaves Medium Foliage. Base the flowers Calypso Orange. Use the #12 flat and Poppy Orange to shade the petals.

2. Deepen some of the shadows with Red Iron Oxide near the center of the flowers.

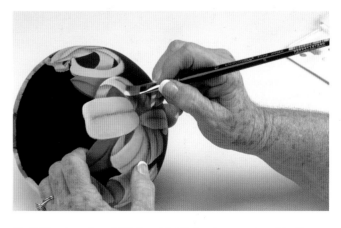

3. Still using the #12 flat, highlight the petals with Butter Cream.

PAINTING THE BOWL

4. Use the liner brush and Georgia Clay to paint the spots on the petals. Start in the center of the flower and work toward the ends. Note that the spots are smaller and sparser as they near the outside edges.

6. To make the water drop, use the #12 flat and Poppy Orange to paint a C stroke, beginning at 12 o'clock and painting counterclockwise down to 6 o'clock.

5. The stamens are a mix of Calypso Orange and White 1:2 with Spice Brown tips. Highlight the tips with Spice Tan where they are on the black background.

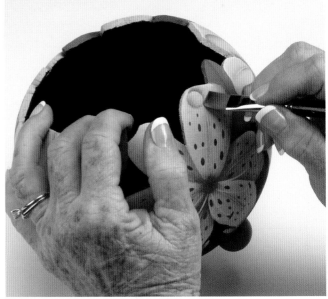

7. Without turning the brush, go back to the top and paint a reverse C stroke clockwise, closing the circle on the clean side.

8. Turn the piece upside down and use White to paint a counterclockwise C stroke on the inside of the circle.

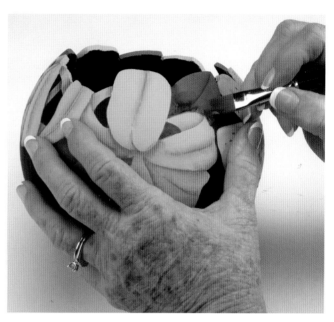

10. Shade the leaves with Dark Foliage using the #12 flat shader brush.

9. Use the liner brush and White to place a comma stroke on the inside on the dark side of the circle.

11. Highlight the leaves with Light Foliage still using the same brush. Paint the feet Medium Foliage and finish with several light coats of spray varnish.

Chocolates Bowl

PALETTE

Delta Ceramcoat
- Roman Stucco
- Spice Brown
- Black
- Mocha
- Dark Chocolate
- Light Chocolate

BRUSHES

Loew-Cornell
- Series 7300 #12 flat shader
- Series 7350 10/0 liner
- Series 7550 1" wash brush

SUPPLIES

- Cannonball gourd, 6-8" diameter
- Craft saw
- 3/16" drill and drill bit
- 3/16" dowel
- 3 ea. 1" wooden balls with 3/16" holes
- Wood glue
- Gloss spray varnish

CHOCOLATES BOWL

CHOCOLATES BOWL PATTERN

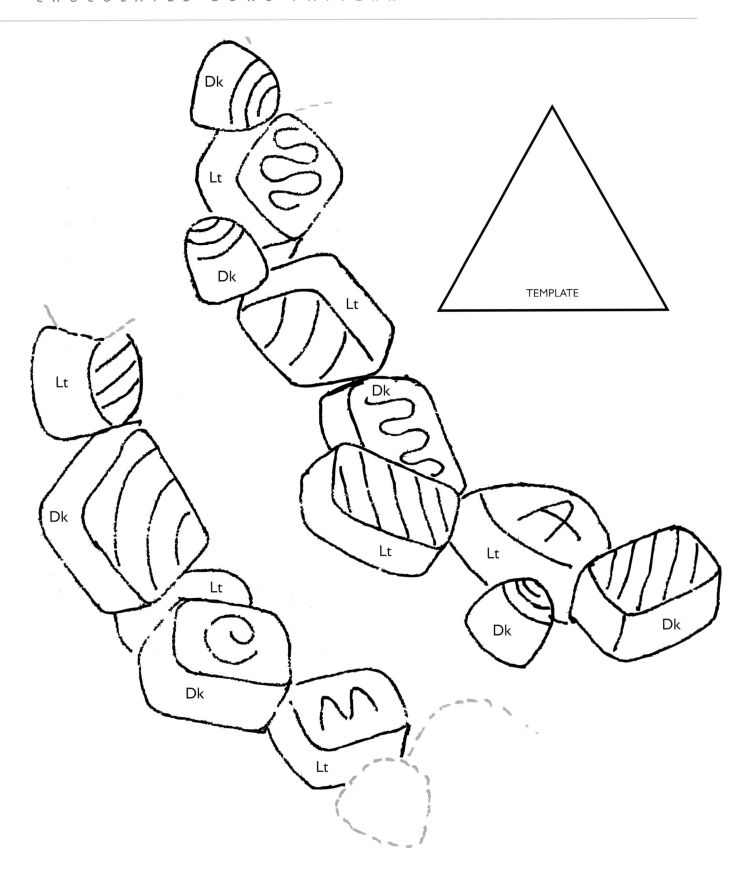

TEMPLATE

ASSEMBLING THE BOWL   PAINTING THE BOWL

Follow the initial instructions as provided in the Introduction "Making the Bowls." Apply the pattern and cut around the tops of the candies.

1. Use the wash brush to paint the inside of the bowl Black and the outside Roman Stucco. Apply the pattern and basecoat some of the candies Spice Brown and some Dark Chocolate. Use the #12 flat and Mocha to shade under all the candies.

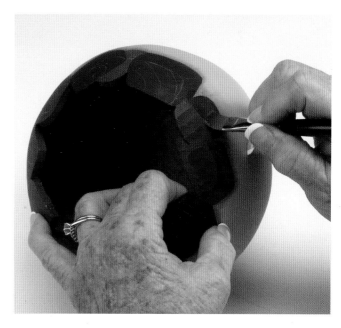

2. Use the same brush to shade the light candies with Dark Chocolate.

PAINTING THE BOWL

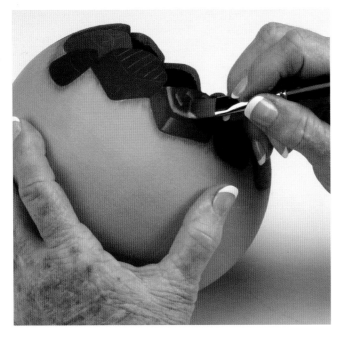

3. Highlight the same candies with Light Chocolate.

5. Use the liner brush and Light Chocolate to highlight the markings on top of the candy.

4. When dry, use the wash brush and wash the entire candy with Spice Brown.

6. Use the #12 and Black to shade the dark candies.

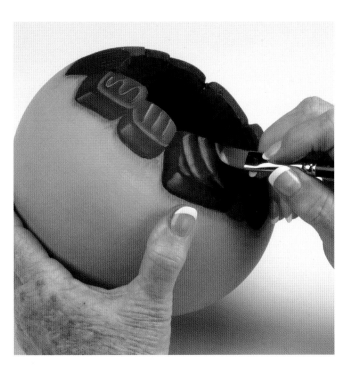

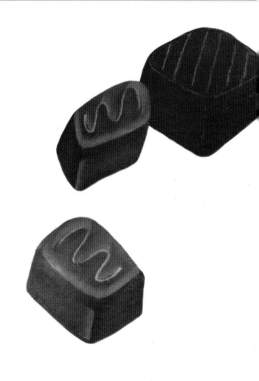

7. Use the same brush and Light Chocolate to highlight.

8. Use the wash brush and wash the entire candy with Dark Chocolate.

9. Use the liner brush and Light Chocolate to highlight the markings on top. Paint the feet Spice Brown and finish with several light coats of spray varnish.

Bats & Moons Bowl

PALETTE

Delta Ceramcoat
- Black
- White
- Rain Grey
- Butter Yellow
- Georgia Clay
- O.J.
- Mocha

BRUSHES

Loew-Cornell
- Series 7300 # 12 flat shader
- Series 7350 10/0 liner
- Series 7500 # 6 filbert
- Series 7550 1" wash brush

SUPPLIES

- Cannonball gourd, 6-8" diameter
- 3 ea. 1" wooden knobs with 3/16" hole
- 3/16" drill and drill bit
- 3/16" wooden dowel
- Craft saw
- Wood glue
- Gloss spray varnish

BATS & MOONS BOWL PATTERN

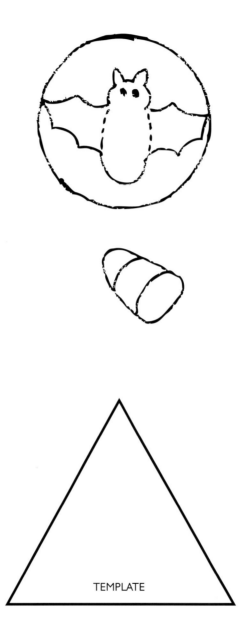

TEMPLATE

ASSEMBLING THE BOWL   PAINTING THE BOWL

Follow the initial instructions as provided in the Introduction "Making the Bowls" and then divide the gourd opening into eight equal spaces. Alter the moon pattern until the moon completely fills each space from side to side and apply the pattern. Cut the resulting scalloped pattern on the edge of the opening.

1. Basecoat the moons and candies White, the feet O.J., and the background Black. Repaint the moons Butter Yellow.

2. Paint the bottom third of the candies Butter Yellow.

PAINTING THE BOWL

3. Use the #12 flat and Georgia Clay to shade all the way around the edges of the moons.

5. Use Mocha to shade down both sides of the yellow and orange sections of the candies.

4. Paint the middle third of the candies with O.J.

6. Use the liner brush and White to apply a stripe down the center of each candy.

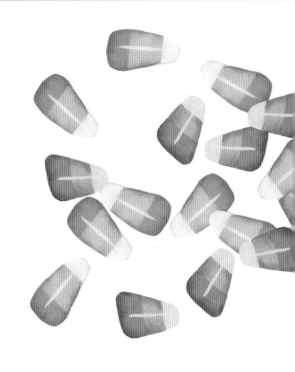

7. Apply the bat pattern and paint it solid Black.

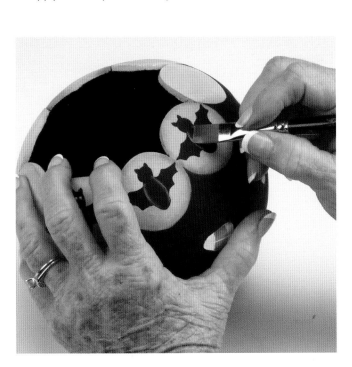

8. Use the #12 flat and Rain Grey to float down each side of the body.

9. Use the stylus and Butter to create the eyes. Finish with several light coats of spray varnish.

Witches' Hats Bowl

PALETTE

Delta Ceramcoat
- Calypso Orange
- Poppy Orange
- 14k Gold
- Navy Blue
- Dark Goldenrod
- Tomato Spice
- Blue Bayou
- Amethyst
- Apple Green
- Black
- Leaf

BRUSHES

Loew-Cornell
- Series 7300 #4, 12 flat
- Series 7350 10/0 liner
- Series 7550 1" wash

SUPPLIES

- 5-7" diameter cannonball gourd
- 3 ea. 1" wooden balls with 3/16" holes
- Drill and 3/16" bit
- Wood glue
- 3/16" dowel
- Craft saw
- Gloss spray varnish

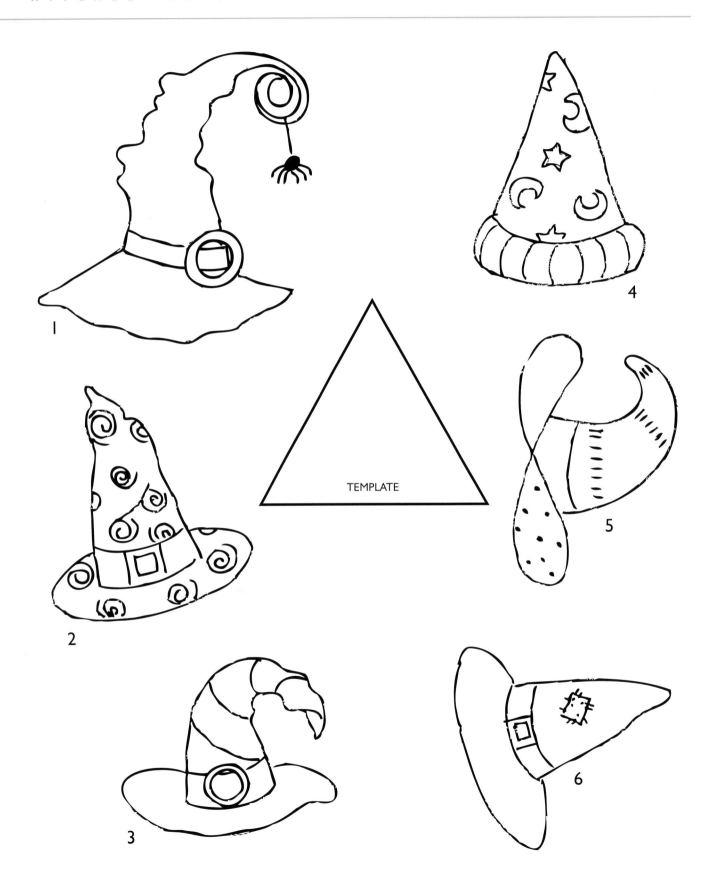

1

2

3

4

TEMPLATE

5

6

ASSEMBLING THE BOWL   PAINTING THE BOWL

Follow the initial instructions as provided in the Introduction "Making the Bowls."

Use the wash brush to basecoat the background Calypso Orange. Apply the pattern and shade under all the hats with Dark Goldenrod.

HAT #1

1. Base the hat Black and use the background for the band. Shade the band with Dark Goldenrod.
2. Paint the buckle Apple Green.

PAINTING THE BOWL

HAT #2

1. Base the hat Poppy Orange with a Black band.
2. Shade the hat with the #12 flat and Tomato Spice.
3. Use the liner brush and 14k Gold to paint the buckle and make the circles.

HAT #3

1. Base the hat Black and use the liner brush and Apple green for the band and stripes.
2. Use the liner and 14k Gold for the buckle.
3. Shade the hatband with Leaf Green.

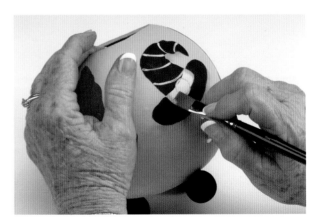

HAT #4

1. Use the #12 flat to base the hat Blue Bayou with 14k Gold stripes and stars.
2. Shade the blue with Navy Blue above the rolled band.

HAT #5

1. Base the hat Amethyst with a Poppy Orange band.
2. Use the #4 flat and Calypso Orange to make the patch.
3. Shade the hat with a mix of Amethyst and Black 2:1.

4. Use the liner brush to add the Poppy Orange stitches to the patch.

5. Use the stylus and Poppy Orange to add dots to the patch.

6. Use the #12 flat and Tomato Spice to shade the hatband.

7. Use the liner brush and 14k Gold to make the buckle.

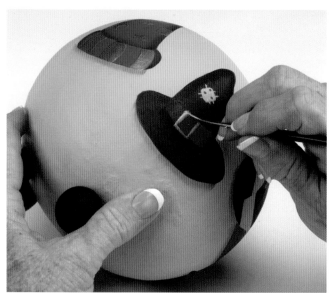

HAT #6

1. Base the hat Black, leaving the hatband Calypso Orange. Underside of the brim is Poppy Orange. Shade the band with Dark Goldenrod.
2. Use the liner brush and 14k Gold for the lines on the crown.

3. Using the same color and brush, outline the hat brim.
4. Use the stylus and 14k Gold for the dots on the brim. Finish with several light coats of spray varnish.

Seashell Bowl

PALETTE

Delta Ceramcoat
- Blueberry
- Custard
- Trail Tan
- Lisa Pink
- Eggshell White
- Spice Tan
- Mudstone
- Spice Brown
- Coastline Blue
- Gleams Pale Gold
- Black

BRUSHES

Loew-Cornell
- Series 7300 #12 flat
- Series 7350 10/0 liner
- Series 7550 1" wash brush

SUPPLIES

- 5-7" diameter cannonball gourd
- 3 ea. 1" wooden balls with 3/16" holes
- Drill and 3/16" bit
- 3/16" dowel
- Wood glue
- Sea sponge
- Gloss spray varnish

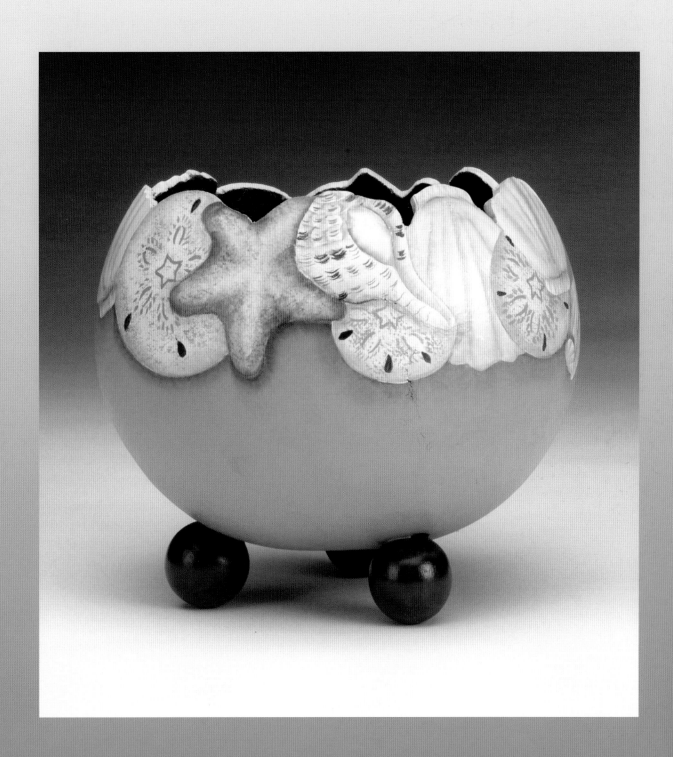

SEASHELL BOWL

SEASHELL BOWL PATTERN

TEMPLATE

ASSEMBLING THE BOWL   PAINTING THE BOWL

Follow the initial instructions as described in the Introduction "Making the Bowls." Apply the pattern to the rim and cut around the tops of the shells. Paint the inside Black.

1. Use the wash brush to paint the background Coastline Blue. Paint the feet Blueberry and all the shells Eggshell White. Paint the starfish Custard and sponge Spice Tan all over it.

2. Shade the edges of the starfish with Spice Brown using the #12 flat.

PAINTING THE BOWL

3. Sponge Custard down the center of each arm to highlight.

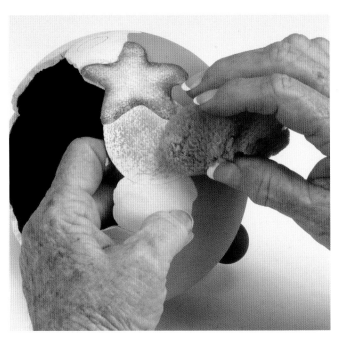

5. Sponge Trail Tan all over the sand dollar.

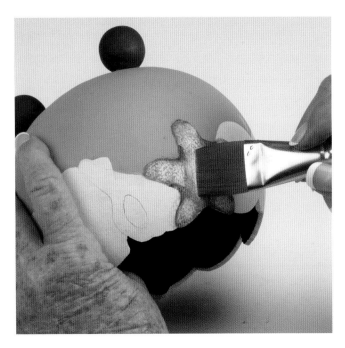

4. Use the wash brush to wash coat the entire starfish with Spice Tan.

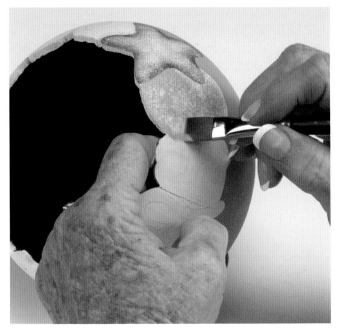

6. Use the #12 flat and the same color to float around the edge.

7. Use the liner brush and Trail to add the details.

8. Shade between the sections of the scallop with back to back floats of Mudstone. Float a little Lisa Pink at the bottom.

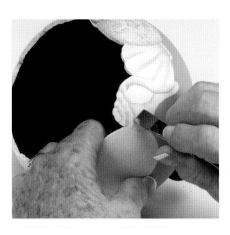

9. Float the sections with Spice Tan.

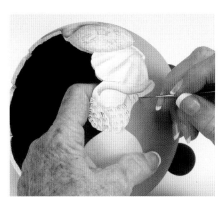

10. Use the liner brush and Spice Brown to make the lines.

11. Float Lisa Pink around the opening using the #12 flat.

12. Use the #12 flat and Blueberry to shade under all the shells.

Christmas Ornament Bowl

PALETTE

Delta Ceramcoat
- Opaque Red
- 14k Gold
- Raw Sienna
- Coastline Blue
- Green
- Spice Tan
- Black
- Tangerine
- Trail Tan
- Blue Jay
- Navy Blue
- Hunter Green
- Spice Brown
- Pearl Finish

BRUSHES

Loew-Cornell
- Series 7300 #12 flat
- Series 7350 10/0 liner
- Series 7500 #6 filbert
- Series 7550 1" wash brush

SUPPLIES

- 5-7" diameter cannonball gourd
- 3 ea. 1" wooden knobs with 3/16" holes
- Drill and 3/16" drill bit
- 3/16" wooden dowel
- Craft saw
- Wood glue
- Gloss spray varnish

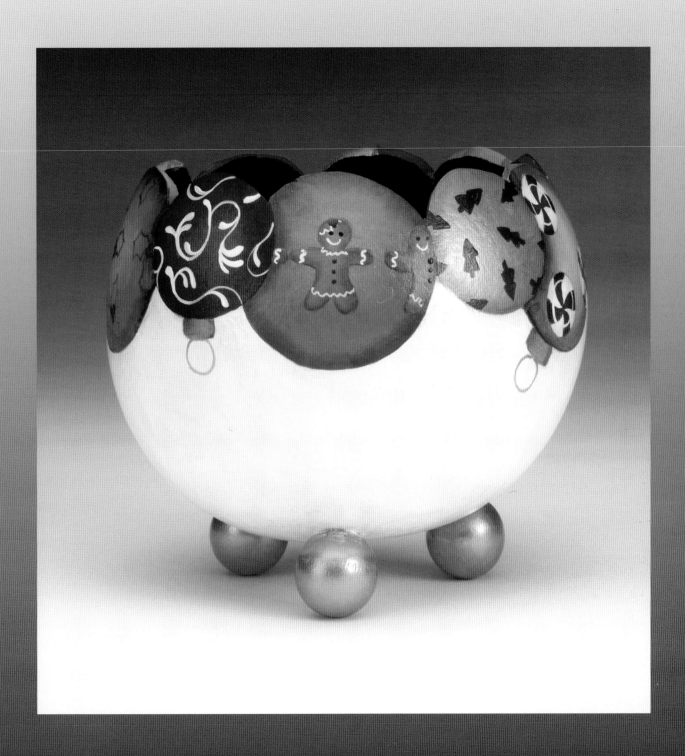

CHRISTMAS ORNAMENT BOWL PATTERN

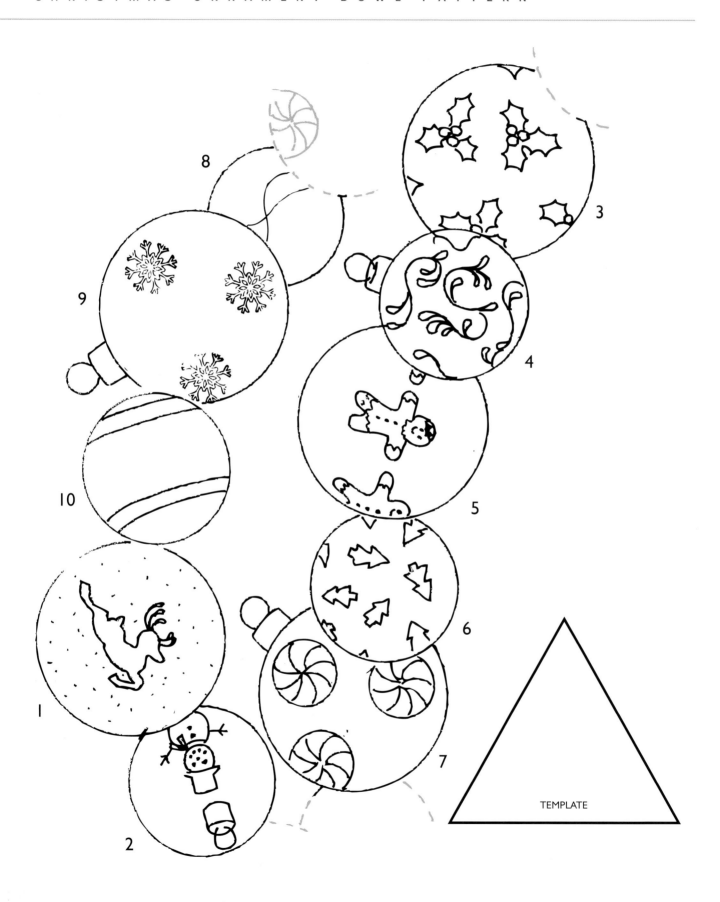

8

3

9

4

5

10

1

6

2

7

TEMPLATE

ASSEMBLING THE BOWL   PAINTING THE BOWL

Follow the initial instructions as described in the Introduction "Making the Bowls."

Use the wash brush and paint the inside Black and basecoat the outside White. Paint the feet 14k Gold. Apply the pattern. After you have painted your ball ornaments (see below), finish with several light coats of spray varnish.

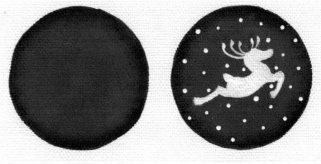

1. RED BALL WITH REINDEER

A) Based in Opaque Red and shaded with Black Cherry all around the edge fading inward. Highlight the center with Tangerine.

B) Use the liner brush and White to paint the deer. Use the stylus for the White dots on the background.

2. BLUE BALL WITH SNOWMAN

A) Base with Blue Jay and shade with Navy around the edges. Wash with the Pearl finish. The cap is undercoated with Trail then 14k Gold shaded with Raw Sienna. All caps are done this way.

B) Use the filbert and White for the snowman. The hat, buttons, and features are Black with an Opaque Red scarf. The arms are Spice Brown.

PAINTING THE BOWL

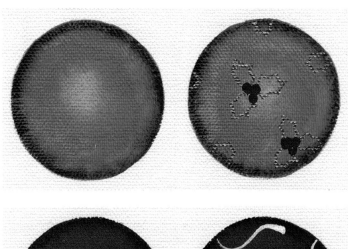

3. GREEN BALL WITH HOLLY

A) Base with Green, shade with Hunter around the edges. Highlight the center with a mix of Green + White 1:1.

B) The leaves are outlined with 14k Gold and the berries are Opaque Red.

4. RED BALL WITH SWIRLS

A) Base with Opaque Red, shade with Black Cherry and highlight the center with Tangerine.

B) Use the liner brush and White to make the swirls.

5. GINGERBREAD BALL

A) Base in Green, shaded with Hunter. The people are Spice Tan.

B) Shade the people with Spice Brown. The trim is White with red buttons and Black eyes.

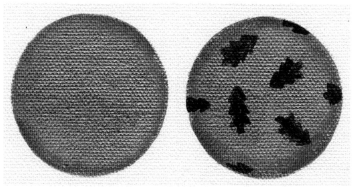

6. GOLD BALL WITH TREES

A) Undercoat with Trail Tan then 14k Gold. Shade around the edges with Raw Sienna.

B) The trees are Hunter Green.

7. PEPPERMINT CANDY BALL

A) Base with Blue Jay shade with Navy and wash with Pearl finish. The candy is White with Opaque Red sections.

B) Shade the white sections with Coastline and the red sections with Black Cherry around the outer edges. The thin White line is done with the liner brush.

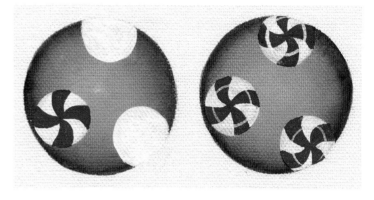

8. RED BALL WITH GREEN RIBBON

A) Painted the same as the first red ball.

B) The ribbon is Hunter Green with back to back floats of Green highlight.

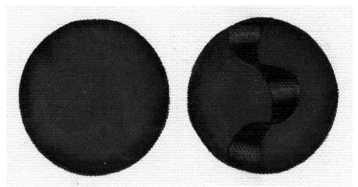

9. GREEN BALL WITH SNOWFLAKES

A) Painted the same as the other green balls.

B) The snowflakes are done with a rubber stamp and thinned White.

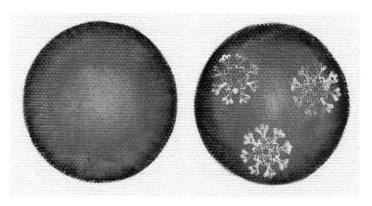

10. GOLD AND RED BALL

A) Painted the same as the other gold ball.

B) The red stripe is Opaque Red, shaded on the edges with Black Cherry with a back to back float of Tangerine across the center. Use the liner brush to make the White stripe.

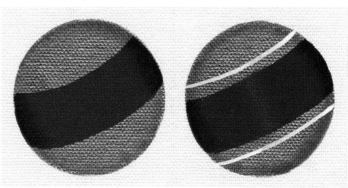

Easter Egg Bowl

PALETTE

Delta Ceramcoat
- Lilac
- White
- O.J.
- Laguna
- Lisa Pink
- Midnight Blue
- Chambray Blue
- 14k Gold
- Pale Lilac
- Mello Yellow
- Orange Pop
- Village Green
- Hydrangea
- Magenta
- Purple
- Deep Lilac
- Candlelight
- Tropic Bay
- Green Sea
- Touch O Pink
- Wedgewood Blue
- Golden Brown
- Black Cherry

BRUSHES

Loew-Cornell
- Series 7000 #4 round
- Series 7300 #4, 6, 12 flats
- Series 7350 10/0 liner
- Series 7850 1/4" deer-foot

SUPPLIES

- 5-7" diameter cannonball gourd
- 3/16" wooden dowel
- Drill and 3/16" bit
- 3 ea. 1" wooden ball with 3/16" holes
- Wood glue
- Craft saw
- Gloss spray varnish

EASTER EGG BOWL PATTERN

TEMPLATE

ASSEMBLING THE BOWL   PAINTING THE BOWL

Follow the initial instructions as described in the Introduction "Making the Bowls."

Follow the directions below for painting each egg. Finish with several light coats of spray varnish.

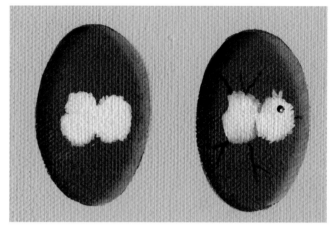

1. PURPLE EGG

A) Base the egg Deep Lilac, highlight the top with Lilac and shade the bottom with a mix of Purple and Black Cherry 3:1. Use the deerfoot and Mello Yellow to stipple the chick.

B) Shade the chick with Golden Brown and add a Black eye. Use the liner brush and the shading mix to make the cracks.

2. YELLOW EGG

A) Base the egg Candlelight, shade the bottom with Mello Yellow and highlight the top with White.

B) The dots are applied with the stylus and are Lisa Pink, Laguna and Deep Lilac.

PAINTING THE BOWL

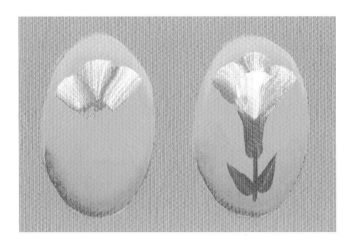

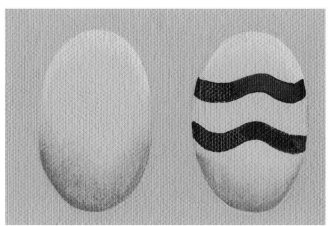

3. AQUA EGG

A) Base the egg Tropic Bay, shade the bottom with Laguna, and highlight the top with Tropic Bay + White 1:1. Use the # 4 round with Lisa Pink & White to make the flower.

B) The stem is Green Sea made with the same brush.

5. GREEN EGG WITH PURPLE STRIPES

A) Base the egg Village Green, shade with Green Sea on the bottom, and highlight with Village Green + White 1:1 on the top.

B) Use the #4 flat and Deep Lilac to paint the stripes.

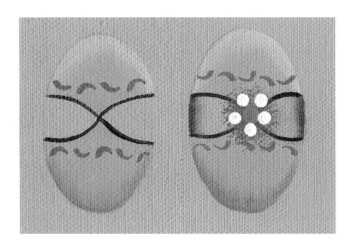

4. ORANGE EGG

A) Base the egg Orange Pop, shade the bottom with O.J., and highlight the top with Orange Pop + White 1:1. The ribbon is Pale Lilac outlined in Deep Lilac. Use the liner brush to make the Green Sea comma strokes.

B) Use the deerfoot to stipple Green Sea in the center of the ribbon and then place a White and O.J. flower over that. Use the brush handle to make the dots.

6. PINK EGG WITH BUNNY

A) Base the egg Touch O Pink, shade with Lisa Pink on the bottom, and highlight with a mix of Touch O Pink + White 1:1 on the top.

B) Shade around the White bunny with Lisa Pink. Shade the bunny with Wedgewood Blue and paint the eye blue also.

7. BLUE EGG

A) Base the egg Wedgewood Blue, shaded on the bottom with Midnight, highlighted on the top with Chambray Blue.

B) Use the #6 flat and Midnight for the ribbon then outline with White dots using the stylus.

9. PINK EGG WITH STARS

A) Base the egg Hydrangea, shade on the bottom with Magenta, and highlight on the top with Hydrangea + White 1:1.

B) Undercoat the stars with Golden Brown then paint them with 14k Gold.

8. ORANGE EGG WITH STRIPES

A) Base the egg Orange Pop, shade on the bottom with O.J., and highlight on the top with Orange Pop + White 1:1.

B) Use the liner brush to paint alternate stripes of Tropic Bay and Laguna.

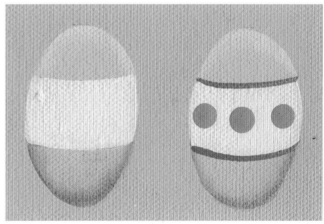

10. GREEN EGG

A) Base the egg Village Green, shade on the bottom with Green Sea, and highlight on the top with White. The stripe is Mello Yellow.

B) Use the liner brush and Wedgewood Blue to outline the stripe and use the end of the brush and the same color to make the dots.

Hearts Bowl

PALETTE

Delta Ceramcoat
- Touch O Pink
- Opaque Red
- White
- Black Cherry
- Chambray Blue
- Coral
- Tompte Red
- Orange Pop
- O.J.
- Village Green
- Lisa Pink
- Bubble Gum
- Pretty Pink
- Tangerine
- Pale Lilac
- Lilac
- Magenta
- Medium Flesh
- Napthol Red Light
- Perfect Highlight for Red

BRUSHES

Loew-Cornell
- Series 7300 # 12 flat
- Series 7350 10/0 liner
- Series 7500 #6 filbert
- Series 7550 1" wash brush

SUPPLIES

- 7-9" diameter cannonball gourd
- 3 ea. 1" wooden ball with 3/16" holes
- Drill and 3/16" bit
- 3/16" wooden dowel
- Craft saw
- Wood glue
- Gloss spray varnish

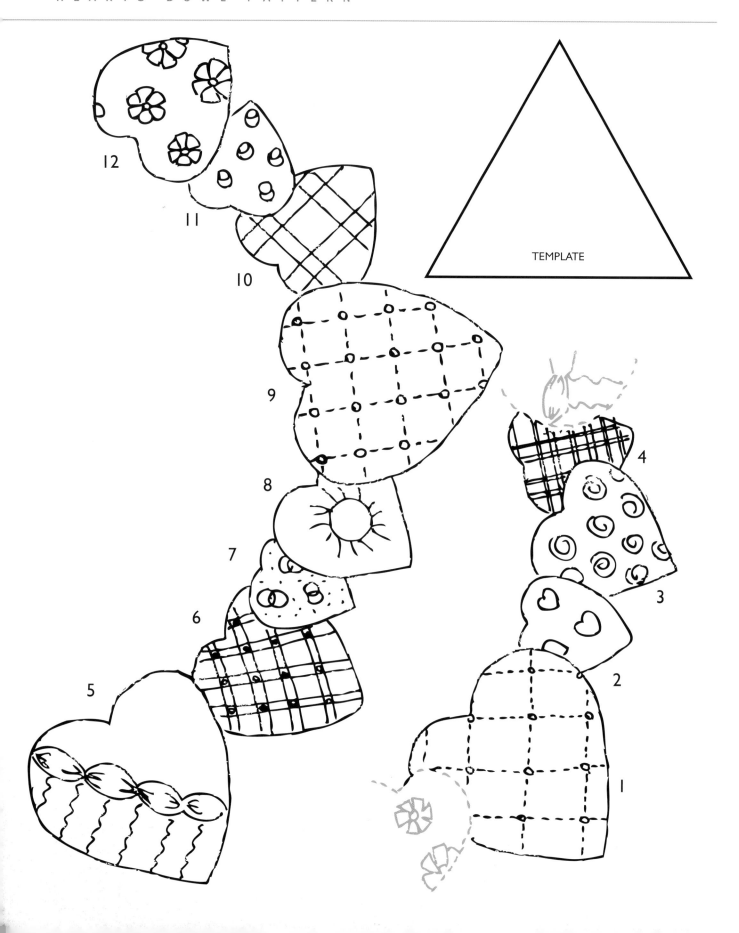

TEMPLATE

12

11

10

9

8

7

6

5

4

3

2

1

ASSEMBLING THE BOWL

PAINTING THE BOWL

Follow the initial instructions as described in the Introduction "Making the Bowls."

Use the wash brush to basecoat the gourd inside and out with Touch O Pink. The feet are Lisa Pink. Apply the pattern.

1. QUILTED RED HEART

A) Basecoat the heart Opaque Red. Shade above the stitch lines with Black Cherry and highlight below the lines with Tangerine. Go over the Tangerine lines with Perfect Highlight.

B) Use the liner brush and Lisa Pink to make the stitches.

2. WHITE HEART WITH SMALL HEARTS

A) Use the #12 flat to shade around the outside edge at the bottom with Chambray Blue.

B) Fill in the hearts with Magenta.

PAINTING THE BOWL

3. PINK HEART WITH SWIRLS

A) Base the heart with Bubble Gum, shade on the bottom with Magenta, and highlight on the top with a mix of Bubble Gum + White 1:1.

B) Use the liner brush and White to make the swirls.

4. PLAID HEART #1

A) Base the heart with a mix of Pretty Pink, Medium Flesh, and Napthol Red Light 2:1:1 and shade with a mix of Coral + Tompte Red 1:1. Use the #2 flat and White for the stripes.

B) Use the liner brush and White for the narrow stripes. Shade with Chambray where the wide lines cross.

5. RED HEART WITH DIAGONAL RIBBON

A) Base with Opaque Red, shade the bottom with Black Cherry and highlight the top with Tangerine, then Perfect Highlight.

B) The ribbon and squiggly lines are White shaded with Chambray Blue.

6. PINK HEART WITH DIAGONAL LINES

A) Base and shade the same as Heart #4.

B) Use the liner brush to make the White lines and the stylus to add the dots.

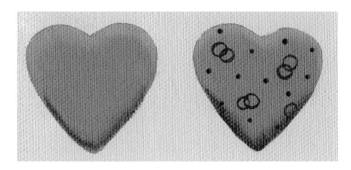

7. PINK HEART WITH DOUBLE CIRCLES

A) Base and shade the same as Heart #3.

B) Use the liner brush and Magenta to make the circles and use the stylus for the dots.

8. RED HEART WITH BUTTON

A) Base, shade, and highlight the same as Heart #1.

B) Use the #12 flat to float Black Cherry around the center and to pull gather lines from the center. Highlight the same as you did the top.

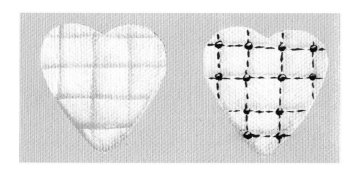

9. WHITE QUILTED HEART

A) Base the heart with White and shade the lines with Chambray Blue.

B) Use the liner and Opaque Red for the stitches and a stylus to apply the dots. Use the liner to place small comma strokes on each dot.

12. HEART WITH FLOWERS

A) Base in White, shade with Chambray Blue.

B) Use the liner brush and Opaque Red to make the flowers.

Do the Conversation Hearts in the following colors:

Orange — Orange Pop with O.J. sides
Purple — Pale Lilac with Lilac sides
Green — Village+White 1:1 with Village sides
White — White with Chambray Blue sides

All lettering on the conversation hearts is done in Opaque Red and the ball feet are Lisa Pink. Finish with several light coats of spray varnish.

10. PLAID HEART #2

A) Painted the same as Heart #3. Use the #2 flat and Magenta to make the lines.

B) Use the liner brush and White to outline the Magenta lines.

11. HEART WITH DOUBLE DOTS

A) Painted the same as Heart #4.

B) Use the brush handle to place White and Opaque Red dots.

Gallery

The finished Chocolates Bowl at different side angles. They look real enough that guests just might reach out and try and take one! See page 12 for project details.

This bowl makes the perfect accessory for your Christmas decorations! See page 38 for project details.

Witches' hats come in all sizes and colors and are a popular part of Halloween costumes! See page 24 for project details.

This bowl is not only great to display at Easter, but you can also keep it out and use it as a great springtime decoration. See *page 44* for project details.

The finished Seashell Bowl at different angles. Which shell is your favorite? See *page 32* for project details.

This Valentine's Bowl is also a great one to keep out and use to brighten the house during spring. See *page 50* *for project details.*

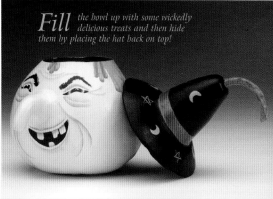

Fill the bowl up with some wickedly delicious treats and then hide them by placing the hat back on top!

Whether full frontal or in profile, this Witch looks just as bad. Which do you think is her better side?

Here are some other wonderful, wicked, and crazy ideas for how to paint and decorate your gourd bowls. The possibilities are endless!

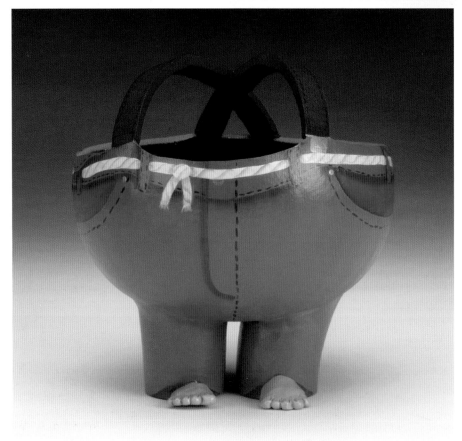